C000126554

Successful
Creativity

in a week

GARETH LEWIS

Hodder & Stoughton
A MEMBER OF THE HODDER HEADLINE GROUP

Orders: please contact Bookpoint Ltd, 39 Milton Park, Abingdon, Oxon OX14 4TD.
Telephone: (44) 01235 400414, Fax: (44) 01235 400454. Lines are open from 9.00 -
6.00, Monday to Saturday, with a 24 hour message answering service.
Email address: orders@bookpoint.co.uk

British Library Cataloguing in Publication Data
A catalogue record for this title is available from The British Library

ISBN 0 340 749237

First published 1999

| Impression number | 10 | 9 | 8 | 7 | 6 | 5 | 4 | 3 | 2 | 1 | |
| Year | 2005 | 2004 | 2003 | 2002 | 2001 | 2000 | 1999 | | | | |

Typeset by Multiplex Techniques Ltd, St Mary Cray, Kent.
Printed in Great Britain for Hodder & Stoughton Educational, a division of
Hodder Headline Plc, 338 Euston Road, London NW1 3BH by Cox & Wyman Ltd,
Reading, Berkshire.

i/n *the Institute*
of Management

F O U N D A T I O N

The mission of the Institute of Management (IM) is to promote the art and science of management.

The Institute embraces all levels of management from student to chief executive and supports its own Foundation which provides a unique portfolio of services for all managers, enabling them to develop skills and achieve management excellence.

For information on the various levels and benefits of membership, please contact:

Department HS
Institute of Management
Cottingham Road
Corby
Northants NN17 1TT
Tel: 01536 204222
Fax: 01536 201651

This series is commissioned by the Institute of Management Foundation.

■■■■■C O N T E N T S■■■■■

■ I N T R O D U C T I O N ■

Creativity is a subject at the heart of many of the most pressing organisational issues such as change, innovation, knowledge based products and services.

In order to survive and prosper in the emerging knowledge economy, we, and our organisations, will need to develop the skills related to understanding, creating and sharing knowledge.

This book should give you ideas and insights into many of the facets of the subject. We will explore why creativity is so important, and what organisations should be thinking about and doing in order to nurture it.

We will look at the personal and psychological aspects of creativity, trying to describe how creative people behave, and how they go about imaginative thinking. We will also set out a range of very practical problem-solving and creative tools that are easy to learn and to remember.

This knowledge is vital because, as the world is changing, so we need to change with it.

This week, we will cover:

Sunday	The creative imperative
Monday	What is creativity?
Tuesday	The creative computer
Wednesday	Being creative
Thursday	Creative problem-solving
Friday	Tools and techniques
Saturday	Creativity in organisations

The creative imperative

> *As tough and uncertain as the digital world makes it for business, it is evolve or die.*
>
> Bill Gates

At the start of the week our key consideration today is:

Why is creativity important?

We need to tackle this question to help us to determine whether creativity is a bonus or some kind of luxury, or whether there are more pressing reasons to be interested in the subject. To do that we will focus primarily on two levels – the level of the individual (that is, us), and the level of the organisation within the context of the economy as a whole. We are going to set out a case that points to the unique combination of factors that make creativity high on the list of priorities for modern businesses and organisations, as well as for individuals.

We will use the following map to help us to navigate this territory:

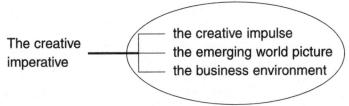

The creative imperative
— the creative impulse
— the emerging world picture
— the business environment

The creative impulse

Before we get down to 'business' we should think of creativity in its historical context. We can be tempted into thinking of creativity as a modern invention, however creativity and innovation have been a component of individual and social behaviour since time immemorial. From the very first attempts by people to organise themselves into more effective social groupings, human creativity has played a critical role in the development of society. Human history is a journey punctuated by an almost uncountable series of creative leaps. Spectacular creative leaps include:

- the invention of the wheel
- the cultivation of crops
- the use of tools
- language
- printing
- space travel.

You could surely nominate many of your own.

1930s   1960s   1990s

If we take almost any aspect of human activity we can trace a long line of development that includes the full range of creative human behaviour and ingenuity to solve problems and make developments. For instance, in agriculture, transport, communications, the written word, food preparation, the visual arts, trade and commerce, manufacturing, houses and homes, health and medicine, leisure and entertainment; and so on. Another aspect of our history is that these creative leaps seem to happen at an uneven pace. There have been notable bursts of creative behaviour. Most of us are familiar with many of these:

- the social, political, military and literary achievements of ancient Greece
- the development of sophisticated cultures and civilisations in many areas of the world – the ancient Chinese, for example
- the sheer scale of human creativity applied in the Renaissance to almost all aspects of human life – trade, visual art, architecture, music
- the use of technology to feed the Industrial Revolution.

For each of these you could name a dozen inventions or discoveries that have substantially improved our lot – see if you can.

Curiosity and the quest for evolution

> *Human beings are not the biggest animals. We're not the strongest or fastest. We're not the sharpest in sight or smell. It's amazing how we survived against the fierce creatures of nature. We survived and prospered because of our brains. We evolved to fill the cognitive niche.*
>
> Bill Gates, *Business @ the Speed of Thought.*

The conclusion from all this is that progress in human and social affairs has always relied on the creative impulses of individuals. Creativity is a component of the way that we

tackle living in the world and dealing with the problems and challenges that life throws at us.

Our basic psychological makeup has not only provided us with a brain, but with a need to use it. We use it to adapt to our circumstances and environment, to control it. Our curiosity and our ability to use our brains to make sense of the world is what distinguishes us from other species. When we add the synergy provided by social behaviour, we have the basic conditions for our creative inheritance.

Human motivation
If we move from the historical perspective to look at ourselves, we also see that our approach to the world involves continuous growth and learning. A look at what we know of psychology tells us a number of things:

1 In the first few years of life babies do some remarkable
   things – they learn to walk and move about; they acquire
   language; they begin to socialise and make relationships;
   they develop cognitive skills.
2 Humans are motivated to seek pleasure and satisfaction
   through physical, intellectual and social means.
3 We retain a need for growth, learning and personal insight
   (what Maslow called self-actualisation) throughout our lives.

What this tells us is that our capacity to learn, to be curious
and to seek to both manipulate the world around us and to
adapt to it is 'wired' into us from birth. In short, it is
impossible for us not to be creative; as these are the key
elements of creativity.

The emerging world picture

Let us now move perspective to the wider world around
us, and in particular the world of commerce and business
that most of us work in.

Although it is obvious that the twentieth century has seen an
explosion of creative energy and activity, it is also easy to see
that we are on the cusp of some dramatic changes at the turn
of the millennium. These changes are visible in a number of
areas, but especially in the economy and in technology.

The economy
In their book, *Blur: the speed of change in the connected
economy*, Stan Davis and Christopher Meyer have charted
three of the most powerful forces now driving major
changes in the economy. They are:

1 *Speed*: The acceleration of all aspects of business – new product lifecycles, time to market, transaction speed.
2 *Intangible assets*: The economy is being driven by non-physical factors. Prices are not based on materials' costs but on intangible factors such as brands, research, marketing, relationships, etc.
3 *Connectivity*: Links are becoming richer, tighter and faster.

This has the effect of blurring the distinctions between product and service, between organisations and their customers and stakeholders, between management and workforce. There are many examples, for instance the website www.amazon.com. Customers who wish to browse the site for information (and value-added services such as book reviews) are also part of the product (when they contribute a book review).

What distinguishes this new economy from the old is intellectual capital – knowledge, talent and experience. This is where the creativity comes in, because if the economy is based on knowledge, then brain power defines the critical skill set.

Technology
Technology is certainly rapidly changing the environment in which we live and work. It is said that we are moving into the information age and, along with it, the knowledge economy.

Consider these facts:

- The Institute for Employment Research in the UK estimates that by the year 2001 nearly 30% of all workers will be in data services.
- Two thirds of US employees work in the services sector – knowledge is becoming our most important product.

- We have seen a substantial growth in Internet connections, e-mail, and trading and working on or via the Internet.

So, as we take these themes and begin to look forward, what do we see?

Ten predictions for the future

1 *Globalisation* – technology conquers distance and organisations can operate anywhere.
2 *Technology* – communication and information transfer is transforming how we live and work.
3 *Social change* – we are entering the information age and the knowledge economy. Manufacturing is becoming marginalised.
4 *Stakeholder power* – organisations are becoming collections of stakeholders.
5 *Innovation* – as a prerequisite for success.
6 *Competitive pressure* – the impossibility of resting on your laurels.
7 *Diverse workforces* – different social mixes (cross-cultural working), expectations (psychological contracts), and working practices (teleworking).
8 *Organisational structures* – more complex and radical architectures for organisations (eg the virtual organisation).
9 *Lifelong learning* – to continually develop our skills, to nurture progress and satisfaction.
10 *Speed of change* – everything is getting quicker.

The business environment

The pace of invention increases exponentially. You only

need to open your eyes and look around to appreciate the overwhelming and massive leaps that have been taken during this century. On first reading it would seem that businesses and organisations on the whole have responded well to meet the challenges created by social and scientific developments. Try this simple test: list all of the products you encounter today that did not exist 5 years, 10 years and 50 years ago.

And yet, for all the weight of history, and despite the fact that we have experienced probably the most innovative century so far, we are not necessarily well prepared for the next. It is sometimes easy to fall into the assumption that business and commerce in the twentieth century has been an unmitigated success.

Organisations in the commercial world have not always been well disposed to capitalise on the creativity of the staff that work in them. How many organisations do you know that you would call genuinely creative or innovative? On the whole, organisations are better at stifling creativity than nurturing it. Although people are clearly naturally creative in the ways that they approach the world around them, this aspect of human behaviour has not always been encouraged or acknowledged by the organisations in which people work.

Most inventions are created within a context and over a period of time. They are rarely accepted at first. There is a process by which they come to fruition. Sometimes that process can unfold in a tortuous and difficult way. We will take just a few examples which will suffice to illustrate the point, even though this has been repeated many times over in the last century. In 1938, Chester Carlson invented the xerographic copying process. Carlson's photocopying process initially failed to generate interest – more than twenty companies turned down his idea. 'I was met with an enthusiastic lack of interest', he said later.

Similar stories apply to many of the inventions that we now take for granted, for example:

- wind-up radio
- post-it note
- Dyson vacuum cleaner.

The stories show how difficult it was for inventors to get organisations to respond, support, promote, or commit to their products. And yet, organisations must face the challenges implied by the changes described in the previous section. The message is simple: innovate or die.

Organisations are now seeking to sponsor and encourage creativity in staff, and to change habits and cultures from those ingrained historical ones.

Gary Hamel is a well known and leading commentator on business strategy and organisational change. He has pointed out that organisations are now more likely to be defined by what they know (core competence) as by what they do. He encourages organisations to focus on the future and on innovation as the primary means of competing or of surviving even.

Our emerging agenda
At the beginning of this first section of the book we posed a question about whether creativity and innovation are desirable or essential. I hope the answer is becoming clearer. Although we can study creativity because it is satisfying and fun, as employees, managers and business leaders we must take the notions of creativity very seriously. The weight of opinion of all those who study and lead changes in our business environment is that we must place innovation at the centre of our thoughts and strategies.

This leaves us with an important set of considerations for the rest of the book:

- Why are creativity and innovation important to my organisation?
- Do I know what it means to be creative, and can I develop a language to talk about it?
- Who is creative, and how do they go about it?
- Are the tools and techniques learnable?
- How can they be applied to real organisational problems and situations?
- How can organisations themselves respond?

Summary

Today, we have tried to set the scene for the rest of the book. Our basic argument is two-fold. Firstly, that creativity is a deeply embedded aspect of the way humans have always tackled the world. Secondly, the emerging world picture is one that will require us to be more, not less, creative in our approaches.

We have set out some simple, but important messages:

- Creativity and the need to innovate is 'wired' into us at a very basic level – it is a feature of who we are and how we live in the world.
- Thus creativity is not new. We have a spectacular history of creative achievement.
- Creative advances in science and technology have provided us with the tools and ideas that in themselves feed the creative merry-go-round of business and commercial life.
- The world is changing. The ways of living and working that we have become used to are about to change hugely and rapidly, and take us into a new era. The pace of that change is also increasing.
- For organisations, the message is simple – innovate or die.
- Traditionally, organisations have not been skilled at nurturing and promoting creativity at work. This will have to change.

What is creativity?

> *[creative attitude] ... first of all requires the capacity to be puzzled.*
>
> Erich Fromm

This may seem an obvious question, but it is not that obvious. Yesterday we looked at why creativity was important in business and working life. Today we shall consider in more detail what it is that people consider creative, and how it comes about. We will also try to develop a richer description of the issues surrounding the topic.

The map for today, then, looks like:

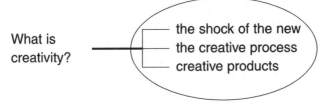

What is creativity?
- the shock of the new
- the creative process
- creative products

The shock of the new

We all think that we know what is creative. Most of us, if asked to identify creative people from the past or present would have little trouble in naming many of the more obvious names, even if we might want to debate the relative merits of each in turn. For example, Leonardo da Vinci, Mozart, Einstein, and Steven Speilberg.

It is an interesting game to play to consider what are the greatest inventions and creative works of human achievement. This particular point in history is a good time to take stock. What would be your own top ten? In *Focus* magazine (April and May 1997) a list of the top 100 inventions was compiled from the votes of readers and the recommendations of a team of experts. Their top five were:

1 *Sanitation*: After 20,000 Londoners died in a cholera epidemic in 1850 it was decided to do something. Cities all over Europe followed suit.
2 *The computer*: The idea was invented by the British mathematician Charles Babbage in the nineteenth century, but the electronic computer was not available for commercial use until after the Second World War.
3 *The printing press*: 1450 Johannes Gutenberg. After this, knowledge became available to all.
4 *Fire*: First used systematically from about 9,000 years ago. What would we do without it?
5 *The wheel*: Presumably derived from rolling logs to move stones possibly about 5,500 years ago.

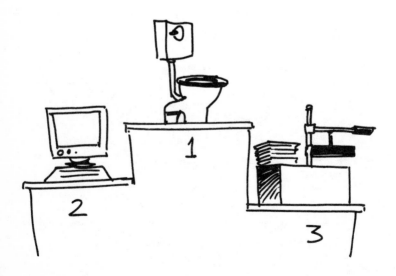

Others that made the top 100 include:

radio (6), antibiotics (7), the internet (8), transistor (9), the laser (10), contraception (12), plastic (14), flight (15), electric light (18), the car (23), maps (28), money (29), telephone (34), photography (38).

Even in the fields of scientific and technological innovation, the twentieth century does not dominate.

By way of contrast, what are the great and lasting creative masterpieces of history? In January 1999, the *Sunday Times* asked this question to its readers. The top five make interesting reading:

1 *Hamlet* by William Shakespeare
2 'David' by Michelangelo
3 'Pieta' by Michelangelo
4 *King Lear* by William Shakespeare
5 The Sistine Chapel by Michelangelo

The top 50 were shared between books and plays, art and sculpture, music, buildings, and one film. Interestingly enough, science and mathematics were only represented by one book – Darwin's *Origin of Species*. Very few works of the twentieth century made it to the list (The Beatles, *Citizen Kane*, James Joyce's *Ulysses*, and Sydney Opera House being among the exceptions).

But creativity does not just reside in a limited number of great works or world-changing inventions. It exists in every area of human activity. There are a multitude of everyday manifestations of what we would generally agree to be creative.

Case study

For those devoted fans of the American cartoon the Simpsons.

Every episode has a different version of Bart writing lines set by his teacher (among my favourites are 'I must not hide the teacher's prozac'; ' Baked beans are not musical instruments'; 'I will not hang donuts on my person').

Every episode has a different creative (sometimes bizarre or surreal) sequence by which the family arrive home and get seated in front of the TV.

We can all have fun recalling our own favourites...

The nature of creativity
Creativity touches many aspects of our thinking, social and acting lives. On page 21 there is a map of the territory, showing some of the important associated concepts.

Even if we just focus on the generation of novel or inventive phenomena, we use a variety of words to describe that aspect of creativity. For instance: produce, create, originate, invent, discover, conceive, imagine, form, construct, think up, ideate, devise, originate, envisage.

This in itself suggests that the single word creativity describes a complex and multi-faceted set of phenomena. Some terms have overlapping meanings and need to be considered separately:

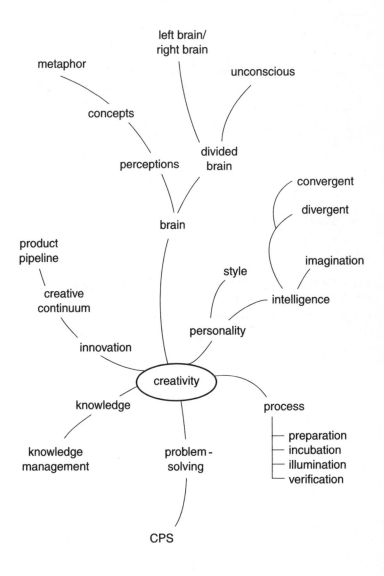

- *Creativity* is producing or bringing something into existence.
- *Creativity*, in relation to a person, is a talent for imaginative creation.
- *Innovation* is the introduction of new things or methods.
- *Discovery* is finding or realising something not known before.

This suggests that there are different ways to be creative, and there are different criteria by which to judge creative outcomes.

For a word that is in such everyday use, there is remarkably little agreement on what exactly it is, especially since we can see creativity and the results of creative acts all around us. It is precisely because of this diversity of human activity and products that it is difficult to tie the word down to a single notion on which we can all agree. It is not only the people and products on which we differ, but on the whole notion of what we consider creativity to be.

Creativity (as opposed to individual creative output, such as works of art) has only really been studied in any depth in the latter half of this century. It is therefore fair to say that our ideas on creativity are really still being formed.

What we consider to be creative is certainly related to some of these attributes:

- newness or novelty
- originality
- uniqueness
- the 'eureka' effect
- the out of the ordinary or atypical
- cleverness.

Here are some of the varying definitions for creativity that have been offered:

- 'Mental processes that lead to solutions, ideas, conceptualisations, artistic forms, theories or products that are unique or novel.' (*Penguin Dictionary of Psychology*)
- 'Any process by which something new is produced – an idea or an object, including a new form or arrangement of old elements.' (Harmon, 1955)
- 'The process of sensing difficulties, problems, gaps in information, missing elements, something askew; making guesses and formulating hypotheses about these deficiencies; evaluating and testing these guesses and hypotheses; possibly revising and retesting them; and finally communicating the results.' (Torrance 1988)

Notice that this last one is a fairly detailed description of a process or sequence of steps.

The creative process

In all the research on creativity, there are between 50 and 60 definitions of the word. They differ in their emphasis on three aspects of the total process:

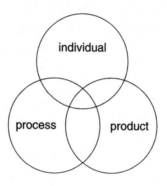

1 *An individual*: There is a person (or in some cases, as we shall discuss later, a group). Their inputs are the thinking skills and the associated ideas that they bring.
2 *A process*: These thinking skills are applied through time, in various stages of a sequence.
3 *The product or outcome*: This is often also in the form of an idea, model, theory or plan (in which case the whole process starts again). It can also be in the form of a tangible result such as a written document, a piece of music, a product, and so on.

The creative individual

As we have already said, it is not too difficult to come up with a list of well known figures, currently or in the past who most would agree were creative. But it does beg some interesting questions:

- Is a person more creative if they write poems in their spare time, rather than play football?
- Are novelists more creative than accountants?
- Would you call your child's first finger painting creative? (Many proud parents, of course, would.)
- Are we all creative or should the term creative only be the preserve of a special few?

There is clearly something special about those whose creative efforts change the world or the way that we think about it. This is sometimes referred to as Creativity with a capital 'C'. However, although there is some disagreement on this, it would be too pessimistic to confine the term creativity to this handful of special individuals throughout history. On the other hand:

Is creativity brilliant conversation? *No.*

Is creativity experiencing the world in novel ways? *No.*

Creativity occurs when the product has been judged to have some value. This implies, though, that the product or output has to be evaluated. How is this done, and by whom? We will explore these ideas below. There are also two further questions, which are important enough for us to consider separately on Wednesday. Are the people who we consider creative different, and how do they do things differently?

Creative products

All the questions above imply that to accept an outcome or product as creative other considerations must be involved. Mihaly Csikszentmihalyi has proposed that creativity is in the interrelations between these considerations. Therefore creativity is a property of a system which is made up of three parts.

1 *The domain*: This is a set of symbolic rules and procedures which make up a body of knowledge. Science, mathematics, visual art are all domains. Each can be broken down into finer grained domains. For our purposes we can also think of examples of more relevant domains:
   - management
   - accountancy
   - mobile communications
   - book publishing
   - retail
   - information services.

2 *The person*: who can apply and transform the body of knowledge into new ideas or patterns.
3 *The field*: This is the set of individuals who act as gatekeepers or judges of new ideas. They are the ones who select ideas and products for recognition. Acceptance can come in many forms:

- management (accepting business propositions)
- customers (who buy or don't buy)
- peers or colleagues
- journals or trade associations (eg the Oscars for cinema).

It is worth saying of course that creativity may be only one of a number of criteria that any of these bodies apply to new ideas or propositions.

This brings us a full circle, because it enables us now to answer the question about what is creative and what is not. The simple answer is that things are creative when they are judged to be creative by the field in question. It gets us out of the dilemma that anything we think is creative must, indeed, be so. It also means that we do not have to be Shakespeare or Michelangelo to be creative. If our domain of choice is paper-folding, we can be creative there if we produce something that is seen as valuable and creative within that fraternity. We don't need an all-purpose set of criteria to apply to any product, as each set of judges (the field) will have a level of agreement as to what constitutes genuine novelty and creativity.

Furthermore, in most domains, there is a natural and continuous process of evolution. This means that ideas, models, theories and products are always changing anyway. They develop new characteristics as people contribute new perspectives and ways of thinking.

Summary

The key points that we have covered today include:

- There is a huge range of things that we call creative – and we have a massive vocabulary to call on. This demonstrates the complexity of the subject.
- We have an everyday notion of what we consider creative behaviour in people, which has to do with being clever or different or off the wall.
- Creativity is a complex phenomenon which involves the individual, the process and the product itself.
- All individuals are creative in their everyday lives, but true creativity involves something more.
- Creativity happens by a sophisticated sequence of stages leading to an outcome.
- Creative products are themselves a system involving three elements:

  – Individual
  – Domain
  – Field

Tomorrow we will go on to look in more detail at what makes creative people creative.

The creative computer

> *Let us learn to dream and perhaps we will discover the truth.*
> Kekule

Most of this week we shall be considering how we use our conscious brain to inform ideas and actions in the world. Today we will look at the brain. It is the factory where our ideas and imagination are formed. Our understanding of how the brain works has leapt exponentially in the last 20 years or so. We will review some of the basic facts and processes involved in the brain, and what they tell us about our creative potential.

Our map for today involves:

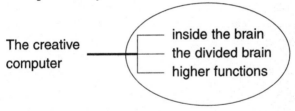

The creative computer
- inside the brain
- the divided brain
- higher functions

Inside the brain

The brain is an incredible instrument. It is mind-boggling in its complexity. It is the processor at the centre of the nervous system. All of the information received from the outside world is processed here, and it generates the signals for all of the other organs and structures in the body to act.

The brain itself is broken down into a number of distinct physical components, some of which are quite primitive and operate the body's systems, outside of our conscious control. The component that we will look at is the cerebral cortex, at the front and top of the brain, which is responsible for many of the higher functions of the brain such as language, thought, processing of sound and so on.

The basic building blocks of the different components are neurons. It is estimated that there are about 10 billion neurons in the cerebral cortex, and that each can have many millions of connections with other neurons. As a neuron can 'fire' up to 500 hundred times a second, that makes an awesome amount of processing power.

In the cerebral cortex, these neurons are collected into groupings that relate to the different functions of the brain. Some of these functions are quite localised. For instance, some kinds of visual processing take place in an identifiable location in the brain. However, other functions such as memory, can be widely distributed throughout the brain, in the cerebral cortex and elsewhere too.

So the physical components of the brain relate to each other and to our conscious cognitive processing in complex and non-linear ways that are difficult to model. This is typical of any complex adaptive system. But it is possibly the most impenetrable that there is. It also poses some questions that are really in the realm of metaphysics – like the relationship between brain and mind; where does consciousness come from, and so on. Such massive complexity makes it difficult to understand in detail how the brain works. In fact, there is almost certainly more that we don't know about the brain than we do know.

It also explains why people over the years have cast around for an appropriate metaphor to assist in our understanding of the brain. Is it a machine? No, it's too complicated for that. Is it a computer? This is nearer the mark, as the brain can be understood as a sophisticated data processing device. However, there are also severe limitations even in this metaphor, as there are many ways in which it does not resemble a computer. This word of caution is necessary, as a metaphor is just that – it is a device that helps us to grasp just some of the complexity by making it simple.

The divided brain

Much effort has been devoted by psychologists and neurologists to understand this modular structure and function of the brain. By using equipment that records the electrical activity of the brain, scientists can relate what is happening in the mind to the activity within the brain. Psychologists study phenomena like perception and memory.

Split brain theory

About 30 years ago, R Sperry, M Gazzaniga and colleagues studied a group of people who had already had the connection (the *corpus callosum*), that divides the two halves of the brain, severed. They observed what happened when the two hemispheres of the brain were unable to communicate. They discovered that these two halves seem to perform different but complementary functions. This idea has been much quoted and much used in books on creativity. In the original formulation, the different halves of the brain were said to work in the following ways:

Left brain
- analytical
- logical
- verbal (the site of language)
- numerical
- sequential

It was seen as being the more conscious, logical brain that controlled our rational processes.

Right brain
- holistic
- pattern-forming
- emotional
- spatial
- musical

It was seen to be the seat of holistic, playful imagination, characterised by ambiguity and metaphor.

Thus the argument went that true creativity involved engaging the right brain, which we were deemed to use

LEFT   RIGHT

very little of in our normal working environment. If only we could be more 'right-brained', then creativity would surely flow. This was a seductive argument, followed by many commentators.

Unfortunately, research since the 1970s has somewhat clouded the picture. The emerging reality seems much more complicated than before, and even the major commentators seem to disagree as to the precise functions of the different halves of the brain.

Whatever the merits of the competing arguments, it seems sensible to accept that there are a large number of sophisticated data-processing and concept-forming functions distributed within the brain, and that creative acts almost certainly involve many or all of them at various stages.

Perhaps we should worry less about the detailed arguments of the academics and accept the split brain theory as a useful metaphor in its own right that serves to remind us of different 'modes' of thought processing that contribute to the creative process.

Also, we shouldn't lose sight of the fact that many sophisticated thought processes need both sides of the brain to fulfil. Understanding jokes is a good case in point, for instance, as it requires you to process information both literally and intuitively.

From visible brain to invisible brain
A distinction that is perhaps just as useful as the left brain/ right brain distinction is the one between the conscious or 'visible' part of the brain, and the less conscious or completely unconscious part of the brain.

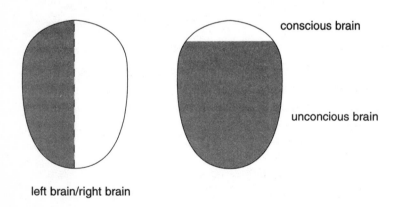

conscious brain

unconcious brain

left brain/right brain

It is fairly easy to demonstrate:

1 that very strange things happen 'down there', below the level of consciousness, and
2 that what happens under (and/or just at the surface) of consciousness is vital in many aspects of creative thinking.

Let us illustrate point one.

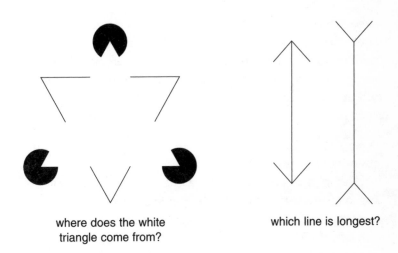

where does the white   which line is longest?
triangle come from?

These optical illusions clearly show that some strange things happen to our perceptions out of our conscious control, and that the reality that the mind produces often bears only a passing resemblance to the reality 'out there'.

It also demonstrates the tenuous relationship between conscious and unconscious processing. However, as we shall see later, this can be used to our advantage.

Higher functions

Creativity is associated with many of the higher level functions of the brain. The spider diagram on page 21 illustrates some of the more important ones. (The relationships illustrated there are entirely personal, and you are invited to re-map them for yourself.)

We will select just two of these to examine their relationship to creative thinking.

Concepts

Concepts are one of the keys to our higher cognitive functioning. They are part of our way of understanding and processing the huge amounts of perceptual information and making it digestible and operable. Our ability to conceptualise is one of the major distinctions between us and others life forms.

But how do concepts come about? They come about through our ability to generalise our experience and sort our thoughts into categories. It should go without saying that we form categories or concepts in highly individualised ways. In itself, it is a function of our creativity that we can do this. The ability to form and re-form information into categories gives us an ever sensitive hold on the world around us.

There is a school of thought: the mathematician Douglas R Hofstadter (who can be considered a school of thought in his own right) proposed that much of our ability to be creative comes from what he calls the 'slippability' of these categories.

Slippability refers to the ability of our concepts or categories to overlap and move from one into another. It might be reasoned that if our ability to make concepts is important then the stronger or more solidly we do this the better – with each concept clearly separated from all others. However, all concepts do have an element of 'fuzziness' at the border. When concepts overlap and merge into each other (to some degree) this can lead to a creative fusion.

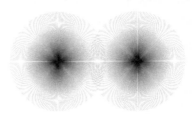

concepts don't overlap –
rigid thinking

concepts overlap –
creative thinking

This can happen quite easily in normal circumstances, although on the whole such overlap of concepts tends to happen accidentally and unconsciously. Malapropisms and Freudian slips are good examples of this accidental creative fusion. For skilled thinkers, the overlap of concepts can also be engineered to some extent to produce variations on concepts and hybrid concepts, and thus totally new ways of seeing the world.

This overlap of categories is a kind of 'twiddling of the knobs' or a making of variations on a theme. It can provide a good explanation for the generation of creative ideas. It might be argued that such 'twiddling' or making variations on a theme is trivial when compared to the titanic ideas we associate with the giants of creativity. Yet these great thinkers on the whole do not think in an entirely different way from us ordinary mortals. The history of great inventions and great works shows that they are all based very solidly on ideas and themes laid down by their predecessors and contemporaries. What they have done is to re-interpret them and re-present them, thus changing the way we see or perceive the world.

Making variations on a theme is the crux of creativity.

The role of intuition
Much of our ability to process and make sense of the data, perceptions, concepts, and so on, under the level of consciousness is called intuition. (It is an interesting aside that a word we all know, used throughout history, only recently has come to have a scientific basis.)

> *Intuition is evolution's default strategy for solving problems.*
> Steven Pinker

There are different versions of the world represented by the division between the conscious and the unconscious. The brain soaks up information, and makes patterns and connections all the time, without you noticing. The result is a body of knowledge that you are not aware of. It can't be verbalised, because verbalisation is in the more conscious aspects of the brain. However, information lost to conscious recall can still influence behaviour and decisions. Furthermore, it seems that we can also learn and recall without being consciously aware of it. It is called implicit learning. As a result of this, people can understand connections and rules that they can neither recall nor verbalise.

This suggests that a good strategy for learning or problem-solving is to put the information and influences in and let the brain do the work. Can it be that simple? Gary Klein, an Ohio-based consultant psychologist has looked at how professionals deal with situations when time is short, the stakes are high, and there is incomplete information. What he has found is that experienced professionals often bypass the more thoughtful, logical and rational decision-making processes. This is fine, of course, as long as the decisions based on intuition are as good or better than those arrived at by more methodical means.

Klein devised experiments where some subjects were asked to take their time and think about it before making a decision, and others were asked for a snap decision. He found that the 'thoughtful' subjects were more likely to change their minds. So what does this tell us? It suggests:

1 that in some circumstances, intuition will serve us very well as it harnesses the unconscious processing power of the brain; and
2 that the brain has an 'implicit' memory and processing system working away out of sight, and there is growing evidence to support this.

In fact, this also makes 'common' sense. A snap decision or an immediate intuitive decision is one where you are using your intuition to access the knowledge that has been stored in your brain quietly over time. The British mathematician and philosopher, George Spencer Brown, summed it up when he said that to arrive at even a simple truth you need years of contemplation, '…not activity. Not reasoning. Not calculating. Not busy behaviour of any kind.'

How often have you heard the phrase 'sleep on it'? We have always valued the invisible processes that are involved in reflection and contemplation.

Yet in modern organisations we are too 'left-brained' – too rational and logical. This leaves little time for altered states and playful approaches, which let the associative and intuitive brain have time to build the connections that it needs.

Summary

What we have done today is to wander over the territory of knowledge about the brain and its functions. This is not a detailed and in-depth exposition of all that is known – that would run to many thousands of pages. We have painted an overview that enables us to draw some useful conclusions:

- The brain is complex and modular.
- Many higher level functions are distributed across the brain.
- We can distinguish between right-brained and left-brained functions, which perform different but complementary tasks.
- In creativity, we also need to be aware of the importance of the conscious and unconscious aspects of the mind.
- Both the slippability of concepts and intuition give us means of relating conscious to unconscious processing in the brain.

Being creative

Originality is simply a fresh pair of eyes
Woodrow Wilson

Today we shall look at creative people. What makes a person creative? What are the processes that are involved in creative imagination? Are creative people different from others? If so, how are they different?

Today's map covers:

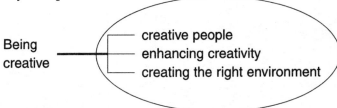

Being creative
— creative people
— enhancing creativity
— creating the right environment

Creative people

Following on from the arguments of Monday, we should be clear that when we talk of creative people, we are not confining ourselves to people who just:

- have unusual ideas
- are interesting or stimulating
- see the world in novel ways
- do or say bizarre or 'off the wall' things.

Rather we are talking about people who make a significant and recognised contribution within their own field.

Life history
One way of delving into the personal nature of creativity is to study the lives and personalities of the geniuses of

history. There have been many studies of the lives of accepted giants from the world of science, music, literature and the arts. We will look at what we know about their personalities from such studies. But first of all, it is worth noting that the lives of many of these people do seem to involve a higher incidence of certain features than the lives of the rest of us. Here are some common features:

- significant loss (particularly of parents) at a young age
- family disruption and dysfunction
- incredibly productive people, for example:
  Picasso – produced over 20,000 works
  Edison – 1,093 patents
  Freud – 330 publications
- not afraid to ask childlike questions, such as Albert Einstein's 'what would happen if I could ride on a ray of light?' which allegedly led him to the special theory of relativity
- intense period of immersion in the domain before major breakthroughs are made
- 'fruitful asynchrony' or being different from the pack.

THE NEXT
BIG THING

THE NEXT
NEXT BIG
THING

THE NEXT
NEXT NEXT
BIG THING

Intelligence

Intelligence was first put forward as a means of predicting educational and life achievement. It was measured in the form of IQ or intelligence quotient. This has turned out to be a difficult concept which has fallen somewhat into disrepute. These days we use the term 'fluid intelligence' to describe a range of cognitive skills important in the more analytical aspects of problem-solving and creativity.

It does seem to be that, on the whole, creative people are more intelligent than the general population. However, the reverse is not also true. That is, being intelligent is not a guarantee that people will be creative. It seems to be that to be creative, you need 'just enough' fluid intelligence.

The 'sister' concept to fluid intelligence is crystallised intelligence, which is that borne of skills and knowledge about the world. You acquire and deepen this over a lifetime. Previously, we have suggested that knowledge and understanding of a domain is an important factor in creative achievement. This correlates with the idea that crystallised intelligence is an important factor in creativity.

Howard Gardner, in his book *Frames of Mind*, put forward the idea that we have a range of intelligences and that we each use different aspects of our creative potential to a different degree. The aspects of intelligence are:

- visuo spatial
- verbal
- personal
- musical
- logico-mathematical
- bodily.

Daniel Goleman says that one of the intelligences is emotional intelligence. Certainly this notion is gathering momentum and support, and would be a good indicator of creativity in social and interpersonal or behavioural contexts.

Personality traits

Creative people come in all shapes and sizes, and that applies to character and personal preferences as well as physical attributes. There are very few traits that seem to apply to all creative people. Are they more extrovert? It seems they are more *and* less. Are they more competitive or cooperative? In fact they seem to be both. This is the contradiction. One thing that seems to set creative people aside is their cognitive complexity. On many of the important scales of measuring or describing human behaviour they seem to be able to move and adapt fluidly from one extreme to the other with more facility than other people. In short, they have contradictory extremes.

Here are descriptions of some of the more interesting contradictions – as set out by Mihaly Csikszentmihalyi in *Flow and the Psychology of Discovery and Invention*.

1 *Energy*: They manage to control their own energy levels being both energetic as well as restful and reflective at appropriate moments.
2 *Intelligence*: They have sufficient intelligence, together with an ability to pose naïve, childlike questions. Certainly creative people tend to have a fluency and flexibility of thought.
3 *Discipline*: Controlled discipline means that highly creative people can move from disciplined perseverance and hard work to playfulness and distance.

4 *Fantasy and imagination*: Again, they are able to move fluently between flights of imagination and rooted reality. Reality can be coped with if it moves and shifts.

5 *Introversion versus extroversion*: They are able to move from being the social isolate to the centre of attention. They have the ability to stand their own company yet be comfortable in the company of others.

6 *Humility versus pride*: They can express the range from arrogance to self-deprecation. This is related to aggressive/ambitious versus selfless/altruistic.

7 *Masculine versus feminine*: They are able to express both aspects of their sexuality.

8 *Independence/rebellion versus tradition/conservativeness.*

9 *Passion versus objectivity.*

10 *Openness versus sensitivity*: They are able to look both outward and inward which means extremes of emotion – pain and pleasure/enjoyment.

Like all such lists, no one person will be able to express the full range of each of these scales. The argument is that creative people are more likely to have a fuller repertoire of behaviour than is average.

Other studies, more grounded in creative behaviour in the working environment, suggest that those considered creative tend to be more:

- tolerant of uncertainty and ambiguity
- self-confident
- unconventional
- original in thought and deed
- intrinsically motivated
- intelligent
- determined to succeed.

Enhancing creativity

How do people apply their skills and preferences in the creative process? As long ago as 1926, Graham Wallas, in *The Art of Thought*, based on his account of eminent creators, proposed a four stage model of creative thinking.

1 *Preparation*: focus on the task and collection of relevant information.
2 *Incubation*: a transfer to unconscious or involuntary work.
3 *Illumination*: when the essence of the problem emerges in a 'eureka' moment.
4 *Verification*: more conscious rational processes used to evaluate the insight.

It is interesting how consistent this is with our views about the importance of intuition and unconscious or 'invisible' processing.

It should not be assumed that these are four sequential stages that must be followed through to achieve success. Rather they show that insight is achieved not by accident but by a combination of processes that include:

* *sorting the wood from the trees* – immersing ourselves in information, and selecting appropriately
* *fitting the pieces of the jigsaw together* – fluidly combining and connecting ideas and concepts, often unconsciously
* *reality checking* – evaluating insights against real world criteria.

On the basis of understanding more about creative people and creative processes, we need to ask how we can use these ideas to help us improve our creative output.

Individual creativity

The discussion above focuses primarily on what people are – their preferences and characteristics. For a moment, we should also think about how they apply both their talents and the approaches discussed. We are what we are and there are some basic aspects of our personality that we cannot change. However, we can practice new skills and we can enhance our repertoire. It seems that there are four things, above all, needed to be a creative thinker:

1 A tremendous amount of information – memory sharpened by practice and positive feedback.
2 A willingness to generate ideas – for fun and enjoyment.
3 A large waste bin – you must be willing to evaluate and to discriminate between the junk and the good ideas.
4 A surplus of energy and attention – you must be willing to devote all your spare energy to your own area of interest.

Strategies for improving creativity
• use all of your brain
• access the unconscious

- reinstate the intuitive
- loosen your concepts – use fluidity
- develop a sense of curiosity – ask challenging questions
- do things you enjoy – and enjoy things you do
- immerse yourself in what you are good at.

There is one final piece of advice that all good creative practitioners have recourse to, and that relates to when and where they are most creative.

Creating the right environment

Archimedes did it in the bath. Newton found it under the apple tree. Where are you most creative? We can take a lead from others who are considered creative achievers.

J Lammiman and M Syrett of Roffey Park Management Institute, in *Innovation at the Top*, studied how and when senior managers and directors were creative.

David Heslop, MD Mazda Cars UK, gets his inspiration in surprising ways. Here are some of them: the way that different essences make a perfume; the way a chef prepares food – care, attention to detail, quality; Zen philosophy; the harmony of music. He says: 'Music is the language which uses creative processes rather than words.'

The perspective of senior managers is shaped by what they read, watch, listen to and experience in private. It is clear from the study that interests outside the workplace influence decision-making. The majority of the best ideas occurred away from the workplace in natural settings such as train or plane journeys, walking, relaxing, playing music. Sport and comedy seem to be featured highly. Here are some of the most mentioned stimuli:

- humour and wit on radio and TV
- networking as a source of stimulus
- talking to passengers on a train
- conversation or contact with colleagues
- 'dreaming and drifting' (this often happens in the oddest places: gardening, opera etc., but can result in breakthrough ideas)
- the community and specialist groups for stimulus and support
- reading – some find inspiration through a fictional character or historical personality
- radio – stimulates the imagination in a particular way
- leisure – renews skills and enthusiasm
- time alone for creative thought.

All achievers are creative in their own particular way. A self-taught chef finds inspiration and wild herbs while running in his native hills in the southern Auvergne. Michael Bras gained the third Michelin star (1999). He learnt cookery from his mother. His specialism is wild and unusual plants. He says: 'I run several times a week in the mountains and it is from these runs that I harvest ideas and emotions.' He finds his inspiration in nature, and hopes to express through his food 'a climate, a freedom of expression, a sense of wonderment, a joie de vivre'. He compares his cooking to jazz, 'for its architecture ... its fluid elegance, its silences'.

> *Source:* 'Michelin honours poetic chef of Auvergne',
> *The Independent*, 2 March 1999

'to sleep, perchance to dream'
There is a wealth of research that shows that sleep can have a positive influence on human performance, and creativity is a component of that.

> *A good night's sleep can make you 40% smarter.'*
>   Harvard medical school

Sleep is also crucial to memory formation and learning. That is, sleep is not passive, it is active in the functioning of the brain. In particular, REM (or Rapid Eye Movement) sleep relates to the cortex of the brain. This is the storehouse of associative memory. It is good at processing context – just like certain aspects of creativity. Good sleep allows us to process facts and perceptions and build them into coherent patterns.

The sleeping brain has been called the 'creative worry factory'. It relies on imagery, metaphor and symbolism. The combination of hard logical working thoughts and the lateral, thinking, dreaming brain enhances creativity. There are many examples of this kind of creative dreaming from the respected achievers of history.

The problem is that in our modern society we are often too busy to get the right amount of sleep. If we are right about the critical role of the unconscious in creative thought, then the role of sleep and deep relaxation may need to be re-evaluated.

Summary

Today we have concentrated on perhaps the most important consideration of all – personality and the functions of the individual brain. These are some of the key points:

1 People who are creative are often:
  - used to adverse or unusual life experiences
  - extremely productive
  - intelligent
  - cognitively complex, and can master contradictions.
2 Skilled thinking involves a sequence that includes:
  - sorting the wood from the trees
  - fitting the pieces of the jigsaw together
  - reality checking.
3 There are mental habits we can develop to enhance our creativity.
4 Creative people engineer the right time, place and conditions for productive thought.

Creative problem-solving

> *Reason can answer questions, but imagination has to ask them.*
>
> Ralph N Gerard

For creativity to be useful in a personal or organisational context it needs to be a cooperative activity applied to real world situations. So today we shall be looking at how to apply creativity within a broader process to tackle real problems.

The map for this section looks like this:

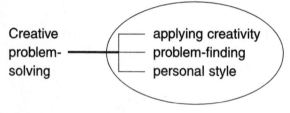

```
Creative             applying creativity
problem-             problem-finding
solving              personal style
```

Applying creativity

There is a strong body of research, based on empirical study of how people tackle real problems, that has developed into a description of the sequence by which substantial problems are tackled. This describes a general framework or a model of the overall process that encompasses all of the sub-processes that need to be involved. It is based on the work of Osborn (the inventor of brainstorming) in the 1950s, developed by Sidney Parnes, and further refined by Isakson and Treffinger, whose approach we use here. Research identified about six separate sub-processes involved in successfully solving problems. These are collected into three main stages:

1 understanding the problem
2 generating ideas
3 planning for action.

At any of these stages, both divergent and convergent thinking processes are involved.

Divergent thinking
This means thinking outwards or widening the options. Successful divergent thinking involves:

* fluency – generating a large number of responses
* flexibility – increasing the scope or the range of different ideas generated
* originality – including the unlikely or unusual aspects of ideas.

Convergent thinking
This means narrowing down the options or selecting specific ideas. It is used to analyse, develop, refine and otherwise evaluate options.

It has sometimes, wrongly, been assumed that creativity is all about divergent thinking. This is a mistake, as rounded and robust creative and problem-solving behaviour is always balanced by the more evaluative and convergent thinking.

The richest and most complete description of the CPS (creative problem-solving) process is shown in the diagram on page 54.

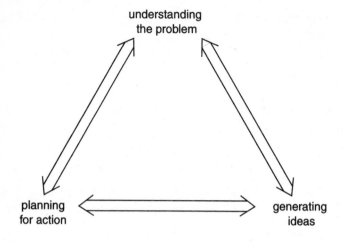

As the diagram above implies, these three primary stages are mutually interdependent. Individual problem-solvers and individual problems may require not only starting at any point, but also moving backwards and forwards through the whole process. The table below does not imply that there are six sequential stages. What it does imply, though, is that robust problem-solving will – mostly – involve activity at all stages.

Divergent thinking	**Convergent thinking**

Understanding the problem

Mess-finding

Seeking opportunities for problem-solving	Establishing a broad general goal

Data-finding

Examining detail from multiple perspectives	Identifying the most important data

Problem-finding

Many possible problem statements	Selecting specific problem statements

Generating ideas

Idea-finding

Producing many ideas	Identifying rich options

Planning for action

Solution-finding

Developing criteria for evaluation of options	Choosing and applying criteria

Acceptance-finding

Evaluating possible actions	Formulating plan for action

If you can think of an example of flawed problem-solving or decision-making in your own organisation you will probably be able to identify from the model the weak or missing stage that contributed to the difficulty.

However, it can sometimes even be an advantage to subvert the process, and come at a problem from a totally different direction. This usually happens when any of the underlying assumptions of a problem are subverted or challenged. Edward de Bono calls this type of thinking lateral thinking.

Murray Gell-Mann, in his fascinating book *The Quark and the Jaguar*, recounts a story of lateral thinking:

Case study

How can you use a barometer to measure the height of a building?
This exam question does have one 'real' answer which the
examiner was, no doubt, expecting. However, the student's
response was to tie the barometer to a piece of string, drop
it from the building and measure. When challenged,
various other solutions were offered. One involved offering
the janitor of the building a 'prize' of a barometer if he
would tell the student the height of the building.

Systems thinking
Specialised problem-solving approaches have been
developed to tackle particular types or classes of problem.
Kepner and Tregoe developed an algorithm to deal with
'deviation from the norm' type problems. They use an
interesting approach to describing problem situations using:

* identity
* location
* time
* magnitude

as dimensions in describing the problems.

More recently a set of approaches has been developed to
tackle open systems or soft systems type problems. These
are situations that are characterised by:

* uncertainty
* ambiguity
* dynamic relationships between components of the system
* feedback from the external environment into the system.

The creative part here is often in the analysis phase of our generalised CPS process. It is required to analyse the systemic structure of the dynamic system. Typical system problems might include:

- stock level fluctuation in supply chains
- supply and demand problems
- the effect of work volumes on quality.

They can be tackled by drawing system diagrams that show the dynamic relationships between the components and variables of the system. They can then be modelled using specialised computer software.

These large-scale systems problems that organisations have to tackle require the development of an enhanced repertoire of analytical and creative thinking skills. These include the ability to:

- seek behind surface data
- obtain data in creative ways
- map relationships between variables
- identify patterns and regularity in situations
- understand cause and effect processes
- draw inferences and conclusions
- map and model systems.

Problem-finding

We have emphasised above that each problem and situation brings with it different requirements. This means in practice that we will approach different problems in individual ways, but there is an implicit suggestion that there are different kinds of problems.

Can we classify or characterise these different kinds of problems? The answer, of course, is yes. And it is important to do so, for two reasons. Firstly, different kinds of problems place different kinds of requirements on us. Secondly, and more importantly, as individuals we will seek out those kinds of problems that suit our interests, preferences and circumstances.

But where do problems come from? Of course, they can come from almost any source, but some typical sources are:

- *The external environment:* forces outside our own organisation or unit can create confrontational situations or the pressure to change.
- *The internal environment:* the need to fix, enhance, improve or update products, services or systems.

- *Our own psychology:* our own preferences and style of doing things, together with our need to manage or control, can create a need to do things differently, or to do different things.

It is a mistake, however, to think that problems come to our attention via a single route. Some problems are there in front of our eyes and can hardly be ignored. Yet others emerge as we immerse ourselves deeper into our chosen domain. There are yet others which we create by virtue of our own interests and perspectives on our working context. For other people they may not be problems at all. They don't arrive by simple recognition, but by us actively seeking new interpretations of current data or by inventing entirely new ways of looking at the world. These give us different types of problem like this:

- *Presented problems*: These are evident in the system, and are recognised by all on the basis of data currently in the system.
- *Discovered problems*: These are implicitly embedded in current data, but need to be discovered by 'digging out' or otherwise probing.
- *Constructed problems*: These are the problems that have the potential to exist, but have to be actively created or invented.

When was the last time you encountered a genuine constructed problem? Try inventing such a problem for your own working environment.

By implication, there is an increase in the creative input required to find and tackle these different classes of problems, as we go down the list. The problems are also more difficult to articulate, progressively further along the continuum from presented problem through to constructed. The latter are the territory of the genuine visionary in a given context or domain.

Case study

In the early 1990s someone had the idea of pre-chopping, washing and packaging lettuce. This was just a bright idea for which there was no historical market. This was a solution for which no problem existed. In 1999 the US market was worth $1.1bn.

If it is possible to do this with a head of lettuce, what's your excuse?   Gary Hamel

Personal style

We have implied that there are significant differences in the way that individuals apply themselves to creative problem-solving in real-life situations. In relation to the CPS some people adopt a linear, orderly progression through the stages. Alternatively, some take a more non-linear complex and random walk through those stages. Added to this, we clearly, as individuals, have our own strengths and weaknesses in relation to different stages of the total process.

Personal preferences and types

One way to get a 'fix' on some of these individual differences is to look at a framework for describing them. One of the most used and most useful frameworks is the **Myers Briggs Type Indicator**. This was based on the work of the Swiss psychologist C G Jung, who observed clear differences in the ways people approached the world, and thus developed his typology. Based on his ideas, the Myers Briggs Type Indicator measures four key scales of differences or preference in individuals.

They are:

Extroversion (E) .... Introversion (I)

This is to do with whether we draw energy from external stimulus (E) or the inner world of thoughts (I).

Sensing (S) .... Intuition (N)

This is the scale of perception. Do we pay attention to hard, concrete facts and details (S) or to pattern, overview or the bigger picture of ideas (N)?

Thinking (T) .... Feeling (F)

This is the decision-making scale. Are we logical, objective and scientific (T), or do we base decisions on more people-centred criteria or values (F)?

Judging (J) .... Perceiving (P)

This reflects our approach to the world. Is it ordered, controlled, sequential (J) or flexible and spontaneous (P)?

Our preferences on these scales will influence our preferences and strengths in relation to problem-solving. In fact, we can draw up the stages of a problem-solving process in respect of the scales.

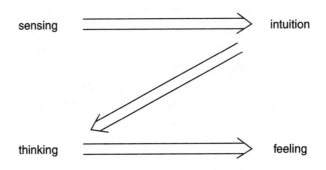

The stages involve:

* Sensing – collecting basic facts and figures, hard data
* Intuition – drawing the facts together, making connections, identifying patterns
* Thinking – rational and ordered decision-making
* Feeling – evaluating options and decisions for consequences and effects on others.

Our preferences on the J–P scale might tell us a great deal about how we approach the total process.

Roles in problem-solving
There have been many attempts to classify and describe the types of strength, style and contribution of different individuals in group and cooperative problem-solving situations. The Belbin team roles profile is one example. The weakness of this for our purposes is that there is an implication that creativity is confined to or concentrated in a minority of the roles.

There are a number of classifications that look at roles specifically in relation to creativity. Edward de Bono's idea of the six thinking hats is quite well known and widely used.

The hats involve participants in a type of mental role playing:

- White hat – an objective look at data and information
- Red hat – feelings, hunches, intuition
- Black hat – logical negative, caution, being judgemental
- Yellow hat – logical positive, feasibility and benefits
- Green hat – new ideas, creative thinking
- Blue hat – control of process

The value of such a framework is that it is simple and it encompasses a good range of creative problem-solving sub-processes, with a balance of convergent and divergent thought. The disadvantages are that it might be difficult to remember which hat is which, and that it can be perceived as artificial.

Summary

Today's section has been aimed at setting out a robust, tried and trusted framework for creative problem-solving. In addition to that we have looked at different kinds of problems and how we arrive at problems in a real working environment.

Lastly, we have considered personal differences and approaches to problem-solving, to allow you to understand your own strengths, weaknesses and personal style.

Tomorrow, we will go on to look at a range of tools and techniques to enhance creative thinking. They can be used, either within a CPS approach, or in their own right.

Tools and techniques

The active process leading to creativity is metaphorical in nature.

Don Faben

Today we are going to look at the range of methods that are available to help individuals to enhance their creativity and to aid in the production of creative ideas.

In order to do this we shall look at:

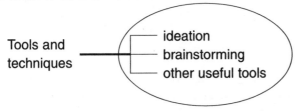

Tools and techniques
- ideation
- brainstorming
- other useful tools

Ideation

Most of the techniques that are around are designed to enhance the production of idea generation. This is because, on the whole, the evaluation components of the creative continuum are to some extent easier and more natural activities. Perhaps this is because they are more 'left-brained'. It is also because people view the ideation stage as being inherently:

- more creative
- more difficult
- less culturally acceptable or 'natural'
- more valuable.

The nature of tools and techniques
However, although we shall also concentrate on the tools

and techniques for idea generation, we shall cover a number of approaches that are more convergent and analytical.

We should note that in relation to these tools and techniques, a number of useful distinctions should be made. The first one is between groups and individuals. Some of these ideas are very much group focused. They are based on the notion that working in groups adds synergy to idea generation. That is, the sum of the parts is more than the whole.

Synergy

$$2 + 2 = 5$$

One of the underlying assumptions is that creative activity is accumulative amongst a group of individuals, so that a group will produce more or better ideas than if the

individuals were to work alone. However, most, if not all, of these techniques can be used individually.

It is interesting to note that creative techniques involve engaging different aspects of our thought processes. Of course, individual differences mean that we use unique combinations of different kinds of processes, but it is also true that different people favour some over others.

On the whole, the different approaches involve some combination of or focus on the verbal, visual and metaphorical.

Verbal
A great deal of our thought processes are based around language. There is a close relationship between concepts and language. Therefore, it makes sense for many people to use verbal techniques to provoke or elicit ideas.

Give your brain a workout by trying to guess what these well known phrases or sayings represent:

1 KJUSTK

2 YOUJUSTME

3 GET IT
   GET IT
   GET IT
   GET IT

4 ie.

5 INVA DERS

You have to dig quite deep for the answers to these, don't you? Did you notice that most of your processing happened under the level of consciousness? The lateral and associative talents of your brain need to be applied, as it is very difficult to arrive at the answers by purely logical, sequential means.

Visual

A picture is worth a thousand words

Most of us live in complex and overloaded information spaces. On a daily basis we can quite easily reach the limit of our brain's ability to consciously process and retain information in a useful form. It is not surprising that we need to develop tools and techniques that help us to cope with this overload. There is a lot of assistance and technology available to enable us to process information once it is organised and externalised. But there is much less help when it comes to the primary information processor available – the brain.

For many people the visual channel is the primary means of dealing with complex, conceptual information. Dealing with large amounts of information and the relationships between the components of the information can only be done visually by many.

Concept Space Maps (or microcosms) are a rich tool for displaying such information. They are a visual arrangement which shows concepts 'in relation to'. They encapsulate large amounts of complex data in a 'mind's eye chunk'. Thus they mirror the natural associative and relational patterns of the brain. Using the power of your visual imagination, microcosm diagrams will help you visualise concepts in this relational way.

We will set out some of the archetypal forms and schemas with which the brain can map conceptual spaces. It takes a little time to learn how to use them because, for some, practice is necessary. However, the benefits are enormous.

The basic format is a simple spider diagram (sometimes called a mindmap), with a natural, associative structure.

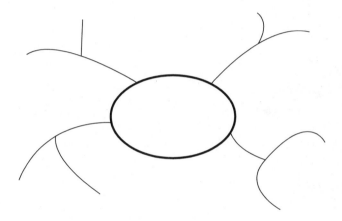

The lines can represent relationships such as:

- breaks down into (hierarchy)
- is a consequence of (cause and effect)
- follows (sequence)
- implies (logical connectivity)
- is related to.

However, it is easy to add structure and order to these in some of the following ways.

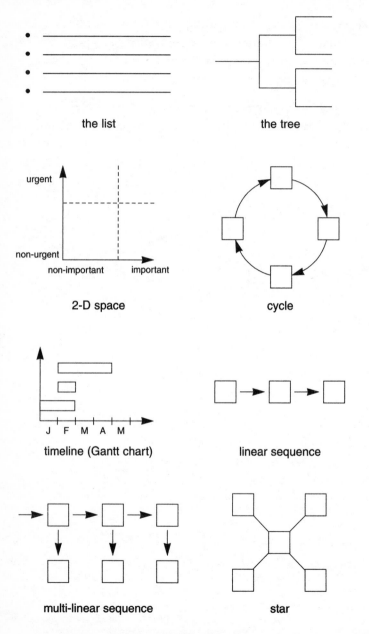

the list

the tree

2-D space

cycle

timeline (Gantt chart)

linear sequence

multi-linear sequence

star

These can be used for recalling, crystallising, organising, summarising or synthesising ideas. They have proved extremely useful in many of the following applications:

- note-taking
- problem-solving
- cognitive mapping (sharing mental models)
- report-planning and writing
- presentations
- process-mapping
- algorithms

Metaphorical

> *We need to understand something of the causal structure of the world.*
>
> Steven Pinker

Because the modern world has grown away from our primitive intuitions about it, we have to invent devices to help us understand it. Analogies and metaphors are powerful ways of doing this.

You do not have to look far in the worlds of science, the arts, culture or society to see how widely we use metaphor and analogy to encapsulate our world. The worlds of management, business and organisations also use metaphor as a means of articulating and communicating identity and purpose.

You may have spotted some of the following things being used as metaphors yourself:

- health
- food
- machines/mechanical

- branching tree
- computing/internet
- chaos theory

Of course, you can also invent your own. They can be very useful for provoking and eliciting ideas.

Case study

I did some training in an organisation which was trying to communicate the importance of customer focus, teamwork, financial results and safety. Because safety was in danger of becoming the 'poor relation' of the four, management used the analogy of juggling the fourth ball – it was difficult but the trick had to be pulled off. The analogy proved a potent tool. Even the chairman, addressing a management forum, mimed a juggle as he spoke about the importance of safety.

Major changes and breakthroughs usually involve a change in the metaphorical backdrop. In fact, by engineering such changes we can achieve the sort of paradigm shift in perspective associated with major change in organisations.

The visual, verbal and metaphorical modes can be used in all of the techniques that follow.

Brainstorming

First and foremost among creative techniques is the idea of brainstorming. It is the one technique that almost everybody knows. It was developed by Alex Osborn in the

1950s. It focuses on the elicitation of ideas. Its main aim is to generate more ideas and better ideas.

The key belief is that we tend to evaluate ideas too early in the formation of creative solutions. Thus we have a habit of killing good ideas at source. This also creates in people an apprehension or a disinclination to go public with their ideas for fear of overly critical comments that reflect on the individual. This has the effect of inhibiting the declaration and flow of new ideas.

Thus the classical approach to brainstorming involves two underpinning ideas. Firstly, ideas are created and recorded without judgement at the initial stage. Any idea is as good as any other. That is, we separate the production from the evaluation. They are separate processes, and their interrelationship is not neutral as evaluation can inhibit production. This separation is the key benefit of the idea of brainstorming as a tool. Secondly, the more ideas the better.

Quantity breeds quality. Brainstorming groups operate a set of conventions:

- criticism is ruled out
- freewheeling is welcome
- quantity is good
- combine and improve where you can.

Only when sufficient ideas have been generated can they be evaluated. There are a number of ways that this can be arranged. For instance, a smaller subset of people or a separate set of people can evaluate. Alternatively, criteria for evaluation can be set and agreed prior to the brainstorming session.

There have been some very strong claims for the benefits of brainstorming as a technique. However, it is not a panacea, and the evidence is equivocal on whether groups produce more or better ideas than a collection of individuals.

The use of brainstorming has been studied by Professors Adrian Furnham and Barrie Gunter. They found that groups performing well structured tasks tend to make better, more accurate decisions. However, they take more time to reach decisions than individuals would. In poorly structured tasks individuals perform better than groups. They are more productive and work faster. It would seem, then, that groups are less efficient than individuals at generating ideas.

However, I think that the value of brainstorming may lie in a different direction. It could be that it provides structure to an activity that is not often legitimated in many organisations – the free reign of ideas, however silly or apparently inappropriate. It provides a framework and it legitimates explicit creative behaviour. It also has a sociological dimension in that it is a way of sharing ideas, sharing meanings, and sharing the outcomes.

One way to improve the productivity of brainstorming groups is to provide a real mix of people, and their skills, approaches and backgrounds. This adds to the 'spark' and widens the scope of potential ideas.

Other useful techniques

Synectics
Originated by William Gordon, this means the joining together of unassociated irrelevant elements. It picks up on the notion that analogy is a natural creative activity. Many accounts of how natural creatives and geniuses go about their work seem to reveal that analogy often comes into it. There are two parts:

1 When dealing with a problem, make a connection between the unfamiliar and the familiar. This is called making the strange familiar. This can be done by asking questions like: *How is a leaf like a snack?* (Answer – *If it's a Pringle*)
2 Secondly, there is a need to look at the problem from a variety of different perspectives. The search for novel viewpoints. This is called making the familiar strange. Ask questions like: *How is a chocolate bar like an animal?* (Answer – *It's a Lion*)

To help elicit ideas you can 'chunk up' and 'chunk down' logical categories by generalising or specifying. So, a crisp becomes a snack, becomes food, and so on.

Attribute zapping

One of the archetypal tests for creativity activities is to find a use for a familiar object. For instance, in the creativity column by William Hartson in the *Independent*, readers were asked to do just that.

Q What can you do with an odd sock?

A Use as a tool to measure right ankles
A Set up emotional reunion with other sock on TV
A Protect cucumbers from frost
A TV show – one foot in the sock
A Cushion for a pogo stick
A Feed it baked beans and use it for a wind sock
A Starch it and use as a boomerang
A Leave it hanging around bars in the hope of picking up some fluff
A Pen pal for Bill Clinton's cat
A 'How can a single sock go walkabout?'

Can you find any others? Try a simpler one:

Q How many uses can you find for a brick?

A way to think up uses would be to look at the attributes of the brick and generate ideas from each one of these. So, for instance, we can describe a brick as:

- red
- rough
- cuboid
- sharp-edged
- heavy
- having two holes.

To create uses for a brick just take each attribute in turn and ask, for example, 'What can I do with the sharp edges?', 'What can I do with the redness?', and so on.

Chindogu
So how do we begin to turn ideas into product?

Chindogu is a lovely transitional idea. It is a Japanese notion that comes from the word *chin* meaning 'unusual', and *dogu* meaning 'tool'. It is a gadget that appears to be useful but really isn't. The rules for a chindogu are that they must be capable of being made, but must not be useful (just nearly useful). It is gratuitous invention, with the main purpose being fun. Here are some rules:

- It must make our life more convenient in some way but must also make it inconvenient in another way.
- It can't be for real use.
- It must actually work.
- It has a spirit of anarchy.
- It is a tool for everyday life.
- It is humorous in some way.

Examples are:

A Swiss army glove – a glove with a tool on each digit.

Hay fever dispenser – a toilet roll holder that sits on the head to dispense toilet roll for hay fever sufferers.

These were some of my favourites, and were invented at a creativity and innovation workshop in Romania.

glass for an alcoholic

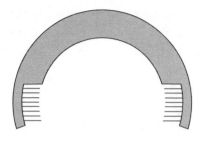

comb for a bald man

The nine-year-old son of a participant in that workshop, concerned about my smoking, invented and offered me this chindogu cigarette! Since we now have such a thing as a commercial comforter cigarette, this one might fail on being too useful. It does, however, show the value of chindogu as a transitional device for getting from gratuitous invention nearer to product.

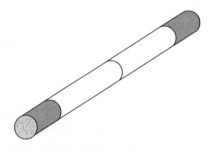

These inventions, no matter how daft they seem, can then be evaluated. Can we see any sense in them? Could they be the spark for any really useful ideas? Because the starting point for chindogus are the little irritations of normal life, and they happen in the stimuli of everyday contexts and settings, it would be quite possible to use real settings, situations or irritations, to begin the process.

For instance, move on from chindogus to look at airline food. We all know it is a problem. But how can we go about inventing a better version? We can do it by listing every aspect of airline food, and questioning, challenging, reversing and reinventing each in turn. We are effectively finding out what 'knobs' our concept of airline food has, and modulating each one in turn. In that way it is quite like attribute zapping.

Attribute – you eat on the plane.

Why? Is it possible to eat before take off?

Attribute – everybody eats at the same time.

Why? What would it look like if we didn't? Self-service?

Attribute – it is delivered on a tray.

Why? Can it be delivered another way? Drinks through a pipe with a personal tap at the seat, perhaps?

In this way, you can take real situations and use them to develop product ideas.

Specific techniques
Certain tools and techniques have been developed to suit specific circumstances. Some that might be useful for further reading include:

- Force field diagrams – for analysing driving and restraining forces in change situations
- Ishikawa (fishbone) diagrams – for problem-solving
- SWOT analysis – for identifying and evaluating internal factors (strengths and weaknesses), and external factors (opportunities and threats) in organisational contexts.

Summary

We have tried to set out today some of the key tools and techniques that can assist in eliciting and developing creative ideas. We cannot cover all of the many (possibly hundreds) of techniques that have been developed for specific purposes or classes of problem and situation. Not everybody will respond to all of these we have presented, but most should find a few that suit their own style of working.

We have considered techniques in the three primary modes of working:

- verbal
- visual
- metaphorical.

We have looked at some key techniques:

- brainstorming
- synectics
- attribute zapping.

Creativity in organisations

> *We don't know who first discovered water, but we can be*
> *sure it wasn't a fish*
>
> Howard George

With this section, we have now come a full circle – to talk about organisations again. Having painted the strategic context on Sunday, we will round off by looking at some key themes and considerations that organisations, and the managers within them, should be heeding. We move from describing the *what* of the situations and imperatives involved, to the *how* of the strategies for dealing with them.

Our map for this involves:

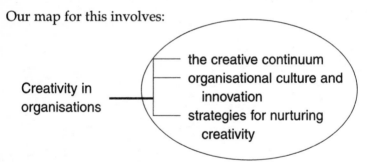

Creativity in organisations
— the creative continuum
— organisational culture and innovation
— strategies for nurturing creativity

The creative continuum

Creative behaviour at work can be difficult for any individual to accomplish. So when we generalise that outwards, to the operation of creativity in groups and teams, and on again from there to organisations, it becomes very complicated indeed. It is a question that touches every aspect of what an organisation is – from its culture, through its systems and architecture, to its products and services.

Creativity (or the lack of it), is not a single problem that can be treated separately and fixed with ease. Creativity in organisations operates in more dynamic, subtle and complex ways.

For much of this book we have talked about ideation. But ideation in and of itself is not enough. There are many examples of great ideas that took inordinate efforts to become successful products. Examples include the tortuous process by which the wind-up radio became a product – with the help of Nelson Mandela. The Dyson bagless vacuum cleaner needed literally hundreds of prototypes to become the finished saleable article.

If even brilliant ideas like this take so much effort, just think how many millions of good ideas are lost on the way. Only an incredibly small proportion of ideas reach maturity and implementation. Even in organisations where there is a sufficiency of good ideas, there can be (and often are) major blockages and hurdles to the realisation of those ideas.

From idea to product
We can conclude from this that there is a linked set of processes involved in the bringing of an idea to fulfilment. We can call this the creative continuum.

ideation ⟹ conversion ⟹ implementation

At the left-hand side we have **ideation** – the generation of ideas.

In the middle we have **conversion** – the intermediate stage where ideas are brought to fruition through design.

At the right-hand side we have **implementation** – where the new product/service is brought to market. It is only if we can move right through the creative continuum that we have genuine innovation.

To study a case, such as the development of the wind-up radio, gives some of the flavour of the persistence and effort (as well as the disappointment) involved in moving from left to right.

The stages are a collection of steps that include:

- a switch from divergent to convergent thinking
- the collection, organisation and verification of information
- various aspects of ideation
- prototyping, model-building, refinement of ideas
- refinement, rejection, reinvention of ideas
- application of reality check, evaluation and validation.

Organisations can be 'mapped' using a diagram like the one below to illustrate their strengths and blockages.

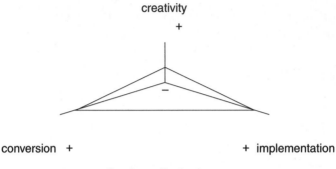

profile of an effective copycat

The continuum is a generalised description. Some sectors have their own quite detailed versions of the same thing. This is particularly relevant for organisations that are heavily involved in research and development or rely heavily on a stream of new products for survival.

The product pipeline
In many industries and organisations these steps are quite
formalised and structured. Take the pharmaceutical industry
as an example. They call the steps from the creation of a
compound to the marketing of a finished compliant product
'the pipeline'. The extreme ends of this pipeline are
characterised as far from market and near to market.

It involves a series of complicated steps including:

- discovery of compounds
- development of drug substance
- development of clinical form
- development of market form
- pre-clinical research
- clinical research
- biostats
- regulatory

Most organisations are not so structured. However, it is
worthwhile looking at the notion of a pipeline. It is
normally easy to guess where ideas get killed in most
organisations, and it is often early on.

Organisational culture and innovation

*The single greatest challenge facing managers in the
developed world is to raise the productivity of knowledge
and service workers. This challenge ... will ultimately
determine the competitive performance of companies.*
Peter Drucker

Organisations need to know how well they are doing. If
creativity and innovation are important, they need to

understand their own strengths and weaknesses. How can they go about doing this?

Auditing creativity
The pipeline is an interesting idea that can help to measure or evaluate effectiveness and efficiency at various stages of the creative continuum. The focus for attention shifts throughout the different stages.

At the left-hand end, the primary focus should be on the organisational environment – behaviour and the enabling culture.

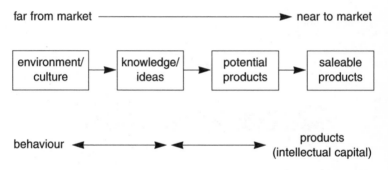

Typical categories to pay attention to here would include:

- effective team-working and collaboration
- professional development
- morale and motivation
- work and management style.

As we move to the right, we become more concerned with outcomes and products – so-called intellectual capital.

Knowledge management
We are just beginning to understand the massive power of

knowledge, but we are at the very early stages of developing tools and processes to manage it properly. There is a consensus that intellectual capital is what knowledge and service workers produce.

There is a 'knowledge pipeline' just as there is a product pipeline. It involves some of the following steps:

- acquisition or generation of information
- transformation of that information into knowledge
- storing and sharing of knowledge
- use of knowledge for innovation.

Case study

According to an Institute of Management survey (December 1997), only 6% felt that knowledge management was just another fad. Over 75% said they felt it was important to organisational survival.

Despite this, 51% said there was no attempt to measure it within their organisation. Failure to capture existing knowledge systematically (78%), a culture of short termism (66%), and a lack of investment in training and development (50%) were rated by managers as the most significant barriers to creating and retaining intellectual capital.

Organisations are going to need to get much better at understanding, managing and enhancing these processes in order to compete for the future. If the message is 'maximise brainpower', then these are the ways in which the organisation can genuinely become a learning organisation.

So where do organisations stand in terms of investment and attention to basic research and development? There are a few clues in the following case study:

Case study

- The Department of Trade and Industry annual Research and Development scorecard shows Britain bottom of the spending league of industrial nations.
- The largest spenders committed 4.4% of turnover to R&D, while British companies spent only 2.3% in 1996.
- Although R&D was perceived as good, design was seen as a luxury or a cost.

This is despite the fact that extra spending on design produces a beneficial increase in turnover and profit. That is, design has an impact on growth. A small increase in design can give a three-fold return. Design-intensive industries tend to grow more rapidly.

Source: *Survey of design activity in British industry for the Design Council, conducted by Centre for Economic Forecasting at London Business School.*

How do management choose among the many new ideas competing for attention? How can the ideas get to be developed? Here are some important considerations:

- Does the management have detailed and comprehensive data?
- Is the data well organised?
- Does the organisation encourage research?
- Does it encourage new ideas?
- Does it disseminate knowledge?
- Is it easy to try things out?

Enabling culture

We have already made the point that culture is an important component of providing the conditions for creativity to flourish within an organisation. But what are the behaviours that enable knowledge to be shared and organisations to learn?

Arie de Geus is a retired Shell executive. He wondered how blue tits managed to discover how to get through milk bottle tops better than robins, especially when, surprisingly, any individual robin was just as likely to discover the trick as any blue tit. The answer is because blue tits flock together, thus communicating the discovery to others, whereas robins are territorial, and if they discovered the trick, they kept it to themselves. We can conclude from this that flocking behaviour promotes knowledge and learning throughout communities. The lesson for organisations is obvious.

Strategies for nurturing creativity

It should be a key priority of management to ensure that creativity is developed and encouraged within the organisation. Creativity is all about individuals. We need to make sure that we have the right people with the right skills. How can this be achieved?

The strategies can be summarised as follows:

1 *Buy them*: Select the right people using the most up-to-date assessment processes, including psychometric testing ideas.
2 *Assess and measure what you have got*: Buy or invent tools and methods for auditing what is important – from culture to intellectual property.

3 *Grow them*: Train people in the importance of creativity and innovation, in the techniques for ideation, in how to develop ideas into products, and in working cooperatively.

4 *Develop management structures and processes*: These need to enable, encourage and reward positive behaviour.

5 *Change culture*: This is the most important of all.

In 1997, the Institute of Personnel and Development commissioned a study, 'The impact of people management practices on business performance'. It showed that people management was critical to business performance, and that financial performance related strongly to high job satisfaction. Good human resource practices had a greater influence on profitability than quality, technology and research and development.

The three key features indicating success were:

• the development of skills
• the developing of a positive attitude among staff
• an empowering culture (autonomy, flexibility, ability to solve problems).

These are sobering thoughts, but if we are serious about innovation, the conclusion from all of this evidence is that organisations must shift their emphasis to the management of knowledge, to learning and to the culture that supports both.

Summary of the week

This week we have covered a great deal of territory.
Creativity is an enormous subject with connections to many
other deep considerations. We shall set out here, by way of
a summary, a set of key questions that will help you review
the week, but also stimulate some further thinking and
learning.

- Do I understand the key forces changing
  organisations?
- What will my organisation and its market look like in
  5 years time?
- How does creativity fit into this picture?
- Can I name and describe creative products from my
  own domain?
- What makes them creative?

- What are the key skills and characteristics of creative people?
- How do creative products come about?
- What creative thinking skills do I have?
- How could I improve them?
- What would help me be more creative?
- What are the key steps in a creative problem-solving process?
- What tools and techniques can I use to enhance my creativity?
- How should I use them?
- Can I evaluate my own organisation's approach to innovation?
- What recommendations could I make?

Further *Successful Business in a Week* **titles from Hodder & Stoughton and the Institute of Management all at £6.99**

0 340 71205 8	Appraisals in a Week	❏	0 340 63153 8	Managing Information in a Week	❏
0 340 70546 9	Assertiveness in a Week	❏	0 340 70537 X	Marketing in a Week	❏
0 340 71197 3	Benchmarking in a Week	❏	0 340 74757 9	Marketing Plans in a Week	❏
0 340 57640 5	Budgeting in a Week	❏	0 340 57466 6	Market Research in a Week	❏
0 340 74751 X	Bullying at Work in a Week	❏	0 340 60894 3	Meetings in a Week	❏
0 340 72077 8	Business Growth in a Week	❏	0 340 74241 0	Memory Techniques in a Week	❏
0 340 70540 X	Business on the Internet in a Week	❏	0 340 61137 5	Mentoring in a Week	❏
0 340 71199 X	Business Plans in a Week	❏	0 340 71174 4	Mind Maps® in a Week	❏
0 340 62103 6	Business Process Re-engineering		0 340 73761 1	Motivation in a Week	❏
	in a Week	❏	0 340 70545 0	Negotiating in a Week	❏
0 340 59813 1	Business Writing in a Week	❏	0 340 64341 2	Networking in a Week	❏
0 340 71200 7	Communication at Work in a Week	❏	0 340 71123 X	Neuro-Linguistic Programming	
0 340 62032 3	Computing for Business in a Week	❏		in a Week	❏
0 340 73781 6	Consultancy in a Week	❏	0 340 73812 X	Office Feng Shui in a Week	❏
0 340 74752 8	Credit Control in a Week	❏	0 340 72073 5	Personal Investment in a Week	❏
0 340 71196 5	Customer Care in a Week	❏	0 340 70541 8	Planning Your Own Career	
0 340 70543 4	CVs in a Week	❏		in a Week	❏
0 340 72076 X	Dealing with Difficult People		0 340 70544 2	Presentation in a Week	❏
	in a Week	❏	0 340 71208 2	Process Management in a Week	❏
0 340 63154 6	Decision Making in a Week	❏	0 340 70539 6	Project Management in a Week	❏
0 340 73762 X	Delegation in a Week	❏	0 340 64761 2	Problem Solving in a Week	❏
0 340 62741 7	Direct Mail in a Week	❏	0 340 73780 8	Psychometric Testing in a Week	❏
0 340 73048 X	E-mail in a Week	❏	0 340 56479 2	Public Relations in a Week	❏
0 340 64330 7	Empowerment in a Week	❏	0 340 71206 6	Purchasing in a Week	❏
0 340 66374 X	Environmental Management		0 340 61888 4	Quality Management Standards	
	in a Week	❏		in a Week	❏
0 340 71192 2	Finance for Non-Financial		0 340 73816 2	Recruitment in a Week	❏
	Managers in a Week	❏	0 340 71198 1	Report Writing in a Week	❏
0 340 71189 2	Flexible Working in a Week	❏	0 340 70538 8	Selling in a Week	❏
0 340 67925 5	Fundraising and Sponsorship		0 340 67397 4	Selling on the Internet in a Week	❏
	in a Week	❏	0 340 65504 6	Statistics in a Week	❏
0 340 71204 X	Going Freelance in a Week	❏	0 340 72494 3	Strategy in a Week	❏
0 340 65487 2	Human Resource Management		0 340 71201 5	Stress Management in a Week	❏
	in a Week	❏	0 340 70542 6	Succeeding at Interviews in a Week	❏
0 340 74287 9	Information Overload in a Week	❏	0 340 71207 4	Teambuilding in a Week	❏
0 340 74756 0	Interviewing in a Week	❏	0 340 70547 7	Time Management in a Week	❏
0 340 71179 5	Intranets in a Week	❏	0 340 71191 4	Total Quality Management	
0 340 63152 X	Introducing Management in a Week	❏		in a Week	❏
0 340 71203 i	Introduction to Bookkeeping		0 340 71195 7	Training in a Week	❏
	and Accounting in a Week	❏	0 340 62102 8	VAT in a Week	❏
0 340 71202 3	Leadership in a Week	❏	0 340 67905 0	Virtual Organisation in a Week	❏
0 340 71173 6	Management Gurus in a Week	❏	0 340 70508 6	Web Sites in a Week	❏
0 340 65503 8	Managing Change in a Week	❏			

All Hodder & Stoughton books are available from your local bookshop or can be ordered direct from the publisher. Just tick the titles you want and fill in the form below. Prices and availability subject to change without notice.

To: Hodder & Stoughton Ltd, Cash Sales Department, Bookpoint, 39 Milton Park, Abingdon, Oxon, OX14 4TD. If you have a credit card you may order by telephone – 01235 400414.
E-mail address: orders@bookpoint.co.uk
Please enclose a cheque or postal order made payable to Bookpoint Ltd to the value of the cover price and allow the following for postage and packaging:
UK & BFPO: £4.30 for one book; £6.30 for two books; £8.30 for three books.
OVERSEAS & EIRE: £4.80 for one book; £7.10 for 2 or 3 books (surface mail).

Name: ....

Address: ....

....

If you would prefer to pay by credit card, please complete:

Please debit my Visa/Mastercard/Diner's Card/American Express (delete as appropriate) card no:

❏ ❏ ❏ ❏ ❏ ❏ ❏ ❏ ❏ ❏ ❏ ❏ ❏ ❏ ❏ ❏

Signature .... Expiry Date ....

Business Checklists titles from Hodder & Stoughton and the Institute of Management all at £8.99

0 340 74292 5	Information & Financial Management	❏
0 340 74290 9	Marketing & Strategy	❏
0 340 74291 7	Operations & Quality Management	❏
0 340 74288 7	People Management	❏
0 340 74294 1	Personal Effectiveness & Career Development	❏
0 340 74289 5	Personnel Policies, Training & Development	❏
0 340 74293 3	Small Business Management	❏

All Hodder & Stoughton books are available from your local bookshop or can be ordered direct from the publisher. Just tick the titles you want and fill in the form below. Prices and availability subject to change without notice.

To: Hodder & Stoughton Ltd, Cash Sales Department, Bookpoint, 78 Milton Park, Abingdon, Oxon, OX14 4TD. If you have a credit card you may order by telephone – 01235 400414
fax – 01235 400454
E-mail address: orders@bookpoint.co.uk

Please enclose a cheque or postal order made payable to Bookpoint Ltd to the value of the cover price and allow the following for postage and packaging:

UK & BFPO: £4.30 for one book; £6.30 for two books; £8.30 for three books.

OVERSEAS & EIRE: £4.80 for one book; £7.10 for 2 or 3 books (surface mail).

Name: ....
Address: ....
....

If you would prefer to pay by credit card, please complete:
Please debit my Visa/Mastercard/Diner's Card/American Express (delete as appropriate) card no:

❏❏❏❏❏❏❏❏❏❏❏❏❏❏❏❏❏❏❏

Signature .... Expiry Date ....